# Flutter - Dart Handbook

# The Developer's Roadmap

Taylor Royce

Copyright © 2024 Taylor Royce

All rights reserved.

# DEDICATION

To those who envision a better world in which technology improves humankind in ways that are still unimaginable.

To the trailblazers that push the envelope of creativity and the unsung heroes who put in endless hours behind the scenes to make the seemingly impossible possible.

To my friends and family, thank you for your constant encouragement and support in all of my endeavors.

And to the readers, whose insatiable curiosity and enthusiasm for learning propel advancement and discovery. You are the one doing this effort.

# CONTENTS

Disclaimer..................................................................................1
ACKNOWLEDGMENTS.......................................................... 2
CHAPTER 1............................................................................. 1
Greetings from Flutter............................................................ 1
   1.1: Flutter: What is it?...................................................... 1
   1.2: Flutter: Why Use It?................................................... 2
   1.3: Introduction to Flutter................................................ 3
   1.4: Hi there, global! Your Very First Flutter Application...............4
CHAPTER 2............................................................................. 8
Unveiling the Dart Language................................................. 8
   2.1: Why Flutter with Dart?................................................ 8
   2.2: Dart Syntax Fundamentals......................................... 9
   2.3: Data Types, Operators, and Variables...................... 10
   2.4: Statements of Control Flow (if, else, for, while)...................12
CHAPTER 3........................................................................... 15
Widgets: The Flutter Apps' Fundamental Components............. 15
   3.1: Knowing Stateful vs. Stateless Widgets.......................15
   3.2: Creating Simple Widgets (Image, Button, Text)................. 18
   3.3: Widget Trees and Layouts......................................... 19
   3.4: Using Flutter to Style Widgets....................................20
CHAPTER 4........................................................................... 23
Working with Layouts in Flutter........................................... 23
   4.1: Configuring Rows and Columns............................... 23
   4.2: Layouts for Stack and Padding................................. 24
   4.3: Center and Align Widgets......................................... 26
   4.4: Complex Layouts with Expanded and Flexible.................. 27
CHAPTER 5........................................................................... 31
State Management Fundamentals.......................................31
   5.1: Comprehending Stateful Widgets and the Construction Process.................................................................................. 31
   5.2: Updating the UI with setState()................................. 33
   5.3: Utilizing User Input (Forms, TextFields)..................... 34

5.4: Using Providers to Manage a Complex State..................... 37
**CHAPTER 6.................................................................................. 41**
**Working with Asynchronous Data................................................. 41**
    6.1: Using the http package to fetch data from APIs..................41
    6.2: JSON Data Parsing...............................................................43
    6.3: Using Widgets to Show Fetched Data.............................. 44
    6.4: Managing Errors and Loading States................................. 46
**CHAPTER 7.................................................................................. 51**
**Navigation and Routing in Flutter............................................... 51**
    7.1: Using Navigator for Navigation........................................... 51
    7.2: Using Push and Pop to Construct Navigation Stacks......... 52
    7.3: Identified Paths and Navigational Debates......................... 53
    7.4: Tabs and Bottom Navigation Bars.......................................55
**CHAPTER 8.................................................................................. 61**
**Animations and Transitions..........................................................61**
    8.1: Comprehending Flutter's Animation....................................61
    8.2: Making Simple Animations using AnimatedContainer......... 64
    8.3: Using Animations and AnimatedBuilder.............................66
    8.4: Producing Personalized Animations................................... 69
**CHAPTER 9.................................................................................. 74**
**Writing Unit Tests for Flutter Apps.............................................. 74**
    9.1: Testing Is Essential to Flutter Development........................74
    9.2: Using a test package to set up a testing environment........ 75
    9.3: Formulating Unit Tests for Logic and Widgets.................... 76
    9.4: Using and Troubleshooting Tests........................................79
**CHAPTER 10................................................................................ 82**
**Deploying Your Flutter App......................................................... 82**
    10.1: Preparing Your App for Distribution...................................82
    10.2: Uploading to the iOS App Store........................................83
    10.3: Introducing Android to the Google Play Store...................85
    10.4: Comprehending App Store Policies................................. 86

# Disclaimer

To the Amazon KDP Team,

Please take note that this book contains code snippets in the write-ups highlighted in dark red. The purpose of including these snippets is to give readers a thorough and hands-on learning experience. They are not meant to result in any unfavorable customer feedback, but they are necessary to comprehend the programming ideas covered. The code is distinguished from the body of the text by the use of dark red, which makes it simpler for readers to follow along and learn efficiently. I appreciate your help and understanding.

Regards,

Taylor Royce

# ACKNOWLEDGMENTS

To everyone who helped to create this work, I would like to extend my sincere gratitude.

To my editor: Thank you for all of your hard work, insightful advice, and determination in helping me to polish my book to its finest. This project would not have been possible without your knowledge and commitment.

I am grateful to my mentors and colleagues in the technology sector for sharing your insights and expertise. Your viewpoints have expanded my knowledge and had a big impact on the book's substance.

To my loved ones, thank you for your unwavering support and tolerance during the composition process. Your encouragement and strength have been a great asset.

I appreciate your interest and inquiry, readers. Your enthusiasm for technology inspires me to investigate novel concepts and disseminate them globally.

To conclude, this work serves as a tribute to the unwavering pursuit of development by all the inventors and thinkers who persist in pushing the frontiers of what is possible. I'm grateful that you've motivated me and a great number of others to envision and build a better future.

# CHAPTER 1

# Greetings from Flutter

**1.1: Flutter: What is it?**

Imagine yourself and your pals enjoying a variety of games on a large playground. Using Flutter, which functions like a magical set, you may design and enjoy any kind of game on your computer or tablet. Google has released a new tool called Flutter that makes it easier to create mobile, tablet, and even desktop applications. These apps include a wide range of functions, including games, drawing tools, and friend chat apps.

Dart is the language used by Flutter. Consider Dart as the unique set of rules that you employ to make your games function. To play games like hide-and-seek or tag, you require rules. Similarly, Dart tells Flutter how to design and function your app.

## 1.2: Flutter: Why Use It?

Perhaps you're asking yourself, "Why should I use Flutter? What makes it so unique?" For the following reasons,

1. One Set for Everybody: Imagine owning a single set of Legos that you could use to construct any kind of structure, be it a spaceship, a palace, or a car. That's how Flutter is. Without writing a lot of code, you can use Flutter to design apps that run on both iOS and Android devices, such as iPhones and Samsung or OnePlus phones.

2. Quick Development: Flutter facilitates the rapid development of apps. It's similar to having an extremely quick assembly line where you can immediately monitor the development of your product. Flutter makes app creation simple and enjoyable by allowing you to view changes instantly.

3. Excellent Designs: Ever find yourself thinking, "Wow, I wish I could make something like that" after viewing an exceptionally lovely image or vibrant game? Using Flutter, you can create stunning applications with vibrant colors,

fluid motions, and animations. Creating an outstanding app visual is similar to having an enormous box of crayons and paints.

**1.3: Introduction to Flutter**

Now, let's prepare to enter the enchanted realm of Flutter! What you need to get going is as follows:

1. A Computer: Windows, Mac, or Linux computers are available for use. Flutter functions with each of them.

2. Flutter SDK: Software Development Kit is what SDK is. It functions similarly to a toolbox that has every tool you'll need to create apps. It is available for download on the Flutter website.

3. An IDE: Integrated Development Environment is what an IDE is. The application where you write your code is unique. Two of the most widely used IDEs for Flutter are Visual Studio Code and Android Studio. They assist you in writing your code and proofreading it.

You're prepared to begin developing your first app after everything is set up!

## 1.4: Hi there, global! Your Very First Flutter Application

The exciting part is about to begin! Now let's create our first Flutter application. Our goal is to develop a basic application that displays "Hello World!" on the screen.

1. Open your IDE: First, launch your IDE (such as Android Studio or Visual Studio Code).

2. Start a New Flutter Project: Usually, there is a way to begin a new project. Choose the Flutter project type.

3. Name Your Project: Assign a name to your endeavor. I'll refer to it as "hello_world".

Your IDE will now configure everything on your behalf. It will take a little while for the new Flutter project to load.

**This is the code that you will begin with:**

```dart
import 'package:flutter/material.dart';

void main() {
  runApp(MyApp());
}

class MyApp extends StatelessWidget {
  @override
  Widget build(BuildContext context) {
    return MaterialApp(
      home: Scaffold(
        appBar: AppBar(
          title: Text('Hello World App'),
        ),
        body: Center(
          child: Text('Hello World!'),
        ),
      ),
    );
  }
}
```

Let's examine the functions of this code:

- Flutter Import: Dart is instructed to use the Flutter library in the first line, {import 'package:flutter/material.dart';`. It would be the same as asking, "Hey, bring in all the tools I need to make this app."

- Primary Purpose: Your app runs in the `void main() { runApp(MyApp()); }}` section. Using the `MyApp` class, `runApp(MyApp())` instructs Flutter to launch your application.

- MyApp Class: You should describe the appearance of your app in this class. With {StatelessWidget`, this portion of the application remains unchanged. It is comparable to a static image.

- Building the App: You provide the appearance of your app to Flutter in the `build` method.

    1. Apps in the `MaterialApp} category adhere to

Google's design guidelines.
2. `Scaffold} is comparable to your app's fundamental framework.
3. The app's top bar, or {AppBar}, is where the title "Hello World App" is shown.
4. The text on the screen is centered by using `Center}.
5. The code that truly displays "Hello World!" on the screen is {Text('Hello World!')}.

You may run your app to see it in operation. There ought to be a play button or an application launch command in your IDE. Upon doing this, an app with the phrase "Hello World!" in the middle ought to appear on your screen.

# CHAPTER 2

# Unveiling the Dart Language

**2.1: Why Flutter with Dart?**

Let's say that Flutter, your magical toy kit, speaks a hidden language that is Dart. Because Dart is so quick and simple to learn—just like learning to ride a bike or play a basic game—Flutter employs it. Flutter uses Dart to create apps more efficiently and fast. It's like having the ideal key to unlock all the awesome capabilities of your app when you utilize Dart with Flutter.

**Dart is a fantastic fit for Flutter for the following reasons:**

1. Dart moves really quickly. It makes your apps operate faster, so when you touch the screen or hit a button, they react instantly.

2. Easy to Learn: Dart is an easy game to pick up and

requires little experience. It's similar to picking up the fundamentals of a new game; once you know how to play, you can go forward!

3. Hot Reload: This amazing feature allows you to see updates to your app right away. Imagine selecting your colors for a drawing and watching them change instantly. Trying out new features in your app is now simple and enjoyable.

## 2.2: Dart Syntax Fundamentals

Let's now examine the fundamental building blocks of the Dart language, which you can think of as the language's ABCs.

- Comments: These are notes that you add to your code to provide clarification; they have no bearing on the functionality of your app. Use // for one-line comments and /* */ for multi-line comments.

    // This is a single-line comment
    /* This is a

multi-line comment */

- Printing Text: The print statement is used to display text on the screen.

print('Hello, world!');

- Functions: Functions are little devices that carry out a single task. A function is something you write once and can utilize as needed.

```
void sayHello() {
  print('Hello!');
}
```

## 2.3: Data Types, Operators, and Variables

Let us now explore variables, data types, and operators in greater detail as we go deeper into the world of Dart.

- Variables: Variables are similar to information storage boxes. It is possible to add, remove, and even modify items within the box.

int age = 10; // This is a box called age that holds the number 10

String name = 'Alice'; // This is a box called name that holds the word 'Alice'

- Data Types: Data types identify the type of information contained in a box for Dart. Typical data types include the following:

for whole numbers (such as 1, 2, 3), int

For decimal numbers (such as 1.5 and 2.7), double

String for text or words (e.g., "Hello").

For true or false values, use bool

double height = 1.75; // A box called height that holds the number 1.75

bool isStudent = true; // A box called isStudent that holds the value true

- Operators: Symbols that act on variables are called operators. Not only can they divide, but they can also add and subtract.

  int a = 5;
  int b = 3;
  int sum = a + b; // sum is 8
  int difference = a - b; // difference is 2
  int product = a * b; // product is 15
  double quotient = a / b; // quotient is 1.6667

## 2.4: Statements of Control Flow (if, else, for, while)

Control flow statements in your application are similar to loops and decision-making tools. They assist Dart in making decisions, much like they do when you play a game.

- If and else statements are employed in decision-making. Take action if something is true. If not, carry out that action.

```
int age = 10;
if (age < 13) {
  print('You are a child.');
} else {
  print('You are a teenager or an adult.');
}
```

- for loop This is used to set a maximum number of repetitions for anything. As if to say, "Do this ten times."

```
for (int i = 0; i < 5; i++) {
  print('This is message number $i');
}
```

- While loop: This continues to operate as long as a given condition is met. It is analogous to stating, "Play until you get tired."

```
int countdown = 5;
while (countdown > 0) {
```

```
    print('Countdown: $countdown');
    countdown--; // This means subtract 1 from countdown
}
print('Blast off!');
```

You should be able to comprehend the fundamentals of Dart's operation. You may now construct basic programs and make choices within your code. Like any game or activity, you'll grow better and better the more you practice. Have fun coding and keep trying new things!

# CHAPTER 3

# Widgets: The Flutter Apps' Fundamental Components

## 3.1: Knowing Stateful vs. Stateless Widgets

Consider using toy blocks to construct a palace. In Flutter, every block is similar to a widget. The fundamental components that make up your Flutter apps are called widgets. Stateless and Stateful widgets are the two primary categories.

- **Stateless Widgets:** Imagine them as unchanging blocks. Like a picture on your wall, they remain unchanged after you set them. They respond to nothing at all, much like buttons that are inert when pressed.

    class MyStatelessWidget extends StatelessWidget {
    @override
    Widget build(BuildContext context) {

```
    return Text('I never change!');
  }
}
```

The text "I never change!" appears in this widget, and it never changes.

- Stateful Widgets are interactive blocks that change based on user interaction. They have the ability to update themselves in response to your actions, like changing the text by hitting a button.

```
class MyStatefulWidget extends StatefulWidget {
  @override
  _MyStatefulWidgetState createState() => _MyStatefulWidgetState();
}

class _MyStatefulWidgetState extends State<MyStatefulWidget> {
  String myText = 'Watch me change!';

  void changeText() {
```

```
    setState(() {
      myText = 'I have changed!';
    });
  }

  @override
  Widget build(BuildContext context) {
    return Column(
      children: [
        Text(myText),
        ElevatedButton(
          onPressed: changeText,
          child: Text('Press me'),
        ),
      ],
    );
  }
}
```

This widget displays a button and some text. The text changes when you press the button.

## 3.2: Creating Simple Widgets (Image, Button, Text)

Let's now explore some fundamental widgets that you will find useful in Flutter.

1. Using a text widget, you can see text on the screen.

    Text('Hello, Flutter!');

2. Button Widget: This is a pressable button. Buttons come in a variety of forms, including Elevated, Text, and Icon buttons.

    ```
    ElevatedButton(
      onPressed: () {
        print('Button pressed!');
      },
      child: Text('Press me'),
    );
    ```

3. Image Widget: This is a widget for showing images. Pictures from your local files or the internet can be

used.

Image.network('https://flutter.dev/images/flutter-logo-sharing.png');

## 3.3: Widget Trees and Layouts

With Flutter, you put widgets together to form the layout of your application. Consider it as constructing a tree, with each widget serving as a branch that supports more widgets. We refer to this as the widget tree.

Widgets labeled Column and Row are used to arrange other widgets either horizontally (Row) or vertically (Column).

- A container widget is a type of widget that resembles a box and can accommodate one child widget. It can have borders, padding, margins, and background colors added to it.

  Container(
    padding: EdgeInsets.all(10.0),
    margin: EdgeInsets.all(20.0),

```
    decoration: BoxDecoration(
      border: Border.all(color: Colors.blue, width: 2.0),
      color: Colors.yellow,
    ),
    child: Text('I am inside a container!'),
);
```

## 3.4: Using Flutter to Style Widgets

In Flutter, widget styling is similar to room décor. You may adjust fonts, colors, and sizes to get the perfect appearance for everything.

- Text Styling: The text's font size, color, and style can all be altered.

```
Text(
  'Stylish Text',
  style: TextStyle(
    fontSize: 24.0,
    color: Colors.red,
    fontWeight: FontWeight.bold,
  ),
```

);

- Button Styling: You can alter the appearance of buttons by styling them.

ElevatedButton(
  onPressed: () {},
  child: Text('Styled Button'),
  style: ElevatedButton.styleFrom(
    primary: Colors.green, // Background color
    onPrimary: Colors.white, // Text color
    padding: EdgeInsets.symmetric(horizontal: 30, vertical: 10),
    textStyle: TextStyle(
      fontSize: 20,
    ),
  ),
);

- Container Styling: You can give containers gradients, rounded corners, and shadows.

```
Container(
  width: 100,
  height: 100,
  decoration: BoxDecoration(
    color: Colors.blue,
    borderRadius: BorderRadius.circular(15),
    boxShadow: [
      BoxShadow(
        color: Colors.black.withOpacity(0.5),
        spreadRadius: 5,
        blurRadius: 7,
        offset: Offset(0, 3), // changes position of shadow
      ),
    ],
  ),
);
```

You may start making your own Flutter apps by mastering these fundamentals, and you can customize their appearance by adding text, buttons, and images. Recall that practice makes perfect, so continue exploring and enjoying yourself while creating widgets!

# CHAPTER 4

# Working with Layouts in Flutter

## 4.1: Configuring Rows and Columns

Say you have a number of toy blocks and you want to stack them on top of one another or arrange them in a straight line. This is accomplished in Flutter by arranging your widgets using Rows and Columns.

- Widgets are arranged horizontally, from left to right, in a row.

```
Row(
  children: [
    Text('I am on the left'),
    ElevatedButton(onPressed: () {}, child: Text('I am in the middle')),
    Icon(Icons.star, size: 30),
  ],
);
```

This example shows a row of text, a button, and an icon placed next to each other.

- Widgets are arranged vertically, from top to bottom, in a column layout.

```
Column(
  children: [
    Text('I am on the top'),
    ElevatedButton(onPressed: () {}, child: Text('I am in the middle')),
    Icon(Icons.star, size: 30),
  ],
);
```

In this instance, the identical widgets are arranged in a stack.

**4.2: Layouts for Stack and Padding**

Widgets can occasionally be stacked on top of one another like sandwich layers, or you can leave room around them.

Stack and padding are useful in this situation.

- Widgets can be stacked on top of one another using the stack layout.

```
Stack(
  children: [
    Container(
      width: 100,
      height: 100,
      color: Colors.blue,
    ),
    Container(
      width: 60,
      height: 60,
      color: Colors.red,
    ),
  ],
);
```

The blue box is positioned behind the red box in this illustration.

- Layout with Padding: Adding padding makes a widget more spacious.

    Padding(
      padding: EdgeInsets.all(20.0),
      child: Text('I have padding around me'),
    );

This text widget appears less crowded since there are 20 pixels surrounding it.

## 4.3: Center and Align Widgets

Occasionally, you may want to ensure that your widgets are precisely centered or aligned a certain way. For this, Flutter offers two specialized widgets: Center and Align.

- The Center Widget positions a widget squarely in the center of its parent.

    Center(
      child: Text('I am in the center!'),
    );

The center of the screen will display this text.

- Widget Align: Align allows you to position a widget in a desired location, such as bottom-right or top-left.

Align(
  alignment: Alignment.bottomRight,
  child: Text('I am in the bottom right corner!'),
);

His text will show up in its parent's lower right corner.

**4.4: Complex Layouts with Expanded and Flexible**

Sometimes you want more control over the amount of space your widgets take up. That's what Flex and Expanded provide you.

- Flex Widget: This unique widget gives you more control over how its children are arranged. However, we frequently use Row and Column, which are based on Flex, in place of utilizing Flex directly.

- Expanded Widget: This type of widget allows it to occupy the remaining space in a column or row.

```
Row(
  children: [
    Text('First'),
    Expanded(
      child: Container(
        color: Colors.blue,
        height: 50,
      ),
    ),
    Text('Last'),
  ],
);
```

The blue container in this example will enlarge to fill the entire area that exists between the two Text widgets.

Expanded functions similarly to a flexible widget, but it allows you even more freedom over how the available space is used.

```
Row(
  children: [
    Flexible(
      flex: 1,
      child: Container(
        color: Colors.green,
        height: 50,
      ),
    ),
    Flexible(
      flex: 2,
      child: Container(
        color: Colors.red,
        height: 50,
      ),
    ),
  ],
);
```

Because the green container's flex is one, and the red container's is two, the red container occupies twice as much room as the green one.

You may customize the layout of your Flutter app by becoming familiar with these layout widgets. Flutter provides you with all the necessary tools, whether you're arranging objects in rows or columns, stacking them, centering them, or allowing them some breathing room. Continue honing your skills and enjoy creating your layouts!

# CHAPTER 5

# State Management Fundamentals

**5.1: Comprehending Stateful Widgets and the Construction Process**

Let's say you own a mystical toy with shape-changing abilities. It may be an automobile, a robot, and finally a plane, for instance. This is similar to utilizing Stateful Widgets in Flutter. As your magical toy changes and updates, so can Stateful Widgets.

- Stateful Widgets: These unique widgets are capable of changing as you work with them. They are able to change their appearance later since they can recall their current state.

    class MyStatefulWidget extends StatefulWidget {
    @override
    _MyStatefulWidgetState createState() =>

```
_MyStatefulWidgetState();
}


class _MyStatefulWidgetState extends State<MyStatefulWidget> {
  String myText = 'I can change!';

  @override
  Widget build(BuildContext context) {
    return Text(myText);
  }
}
```

Here is an example where MyStatefulWidget is not fixed. It is tracked by the _MyStatefulWidgetState class.

- **Build Method:** The build method instructs Flutter on how to draw your widget on the screen, just like a blueprint would. Flutter updates the screen by making another call to the build function whenever the widget changes.

## 5.2: Updating the UI with setState()

Let's now explore how to modify your Stateful Widget. You employ setState(), a unique technique.

Flutter is informed, "Hey, something has changed!" using setState(). Update the screen, please. It's similar to turning your magical toy from a car to a robot by simply hitting a button.

```
class MyStatefulWidget extends StatefulWidget {
  @override
  _MyStatefulWidgetState createState() => _MyStatefulWidgetState();
}

class _MyStatefulWidgetState extends State<MyStatefulWidget> {
  String myText = 'Press the button to change me!';

  void changeText() {
    setState(() {
      myText = 'I have changed!';
```

      });
    }

    @override
    Widget build(BuildContext context) {
      return Column(
        children: [
          Text(myText),
          ElevatedButton(
            onPressed: changeText,
            child: Text('Press me'),
          ),
        ],
      );
    }
}

In this example, the changeText function calls setState(), which modifies the text on the screen, when you hit the button.

**5.3: Utilizing User Input (Forms, TextFields)**

Sometimes you want the user to enter data into your app—for example, by filling out a form or entering in their name.

- TextField Widget: With this widget, text entry is possible.

  ```
  TextField(
    onChanged: (text) {
      print('You typed: $text');
    },
  );
  ```

- Forms: A collection of TextFields that you can handle collectively is called a Form. It is employed to gather user feedback.

  ```
  class MyForm extends StatefulWidget {
    @override
    _MyFormState createState() => _MyFormState();
  }

  class _MyFormState extends State<MyForm> {
  ```

```dart
final _formKey = GlobalKey<FormState>();
String _name = '';

@override
Widget build(BuildContext context) {
  return Form(
    key: _formKey,
    child: Column(
      children: [
        TextFormField(
          decoration: InputDecoration(labelText: 'Enter your name'),
          onSaved: (value) {
            _name = value ?? '';
          },
        ),
        ElevatedButton(
          onPressed: () {
            if (_formKey.currentState?.validate() ?? false) {
              _formKey.currentState?.save();
              print('Your name is $_name');
            }
```

```
          },
          child: Text('Submit'),
        ),
      ],
    ),
  );
 }
}
```

In this example, when the button is pressed, the form gathers the user's name and prints it.

## 5.4: Using Providers to Manage a Complex State

Keeping your app's state under control might get challenging as it grows in size. Here's where the useful tool known as Provider comes in. Provider facilitates your clean and simple management of complicated conditions.

- Provider: Picture Provider as a magical assistant that simplifies the sharing and management of state among various app components.

```dart
class Counter with ChangeNotifier {
  int _count = 0;

  int get count => _count;

  void increment() {
    _count++;
    notifyListeners();
  }
}

void main() {
  runApp(
    ChangeNotifierProvider(
      create: (context) => Counter(),
      child: MyApp(),
    ),
  );
}

class MyApp extends StatelessWidget {
  @override
  Widget build(BuildContext context) {
```

```
return MaterialApp(
  home: Scaffold(
    appBar: AppBar(title: Text('Provider Example')),
    body: Center(
      child: Column(
        mainAxisAlignment: MainAxisAlignment.center,
        children: [
          Text('You have pressed the button this many times:'),
          Consumer<Counter>(
            builder: (context, counter, child) {
              return Text('${counter.count}');
            },
          ),
        ],
      ),
    ),
    floatingActionButton: FloatingActionButton(
      onPressed: () {
        Provider.of<Counter>(context, listen: false).increment();
```

```
        },
      child: Icon(Icons.add),
    ),
   ),
  );
 }
}
```

In this instance, a count is monitored by the Counter class. Accessing and updating this count is made simple by the Provider from anywhere within the app. The UI immediately refreshes and the count rises when you press the button.

You may add interactivity and dynamic elements to your Flutter apps by grasping these fundamentals of state management. It's simple to refresh the user interface, handle user input, and maintain complicated states. Try and practice more till you have the feel of it. Have fun with coding!

# CHAPTER 6

# Working with Asynchronous Data

**6.1: Using the http package to fetch data from APIs**

Consider that you would like to receive the most recent news or weather data for your app. Usually, this data is saved online, so you'll need to retrieve it. In Flutter, we obtain this data through the usage of an API. An API functions similarly to a waiter who brings you the meal you requested at a restaurant. The http package can be used to retrieve data from an API.

- Installing the http package: Your project must first have the http package installed. This package facilitates API communication.

    dependencies:
      http: ^0.13.3

Run flutter pub to install the package after adding this.

- **Data Fetching:** Let's build some code at this point to retrieve data from an API.

  ```
  import 'package:http/http.dart' as http;

  Future<String> fetchData() async {
      final response = await http.get(Uri.parse('https://jsonplaceholder.typicode.com/todos/1'));

    if (response.statusCode == 200) {
      return response.body;
    } else {
      throw Exception('Failed to load data');
    }
  }
  ```

We are retrieving data from a sample API in this instance. We return the data in the event that the request is successful (status code 200). If not, an error is thrown.

## 6.2: JSON Data Parsing

The format that data arrives in when it is fetched via an API is often JSON (JavaScript Object Notation). JSON is similar to a format for writing data that is simple enough for computers and people to comprehend. However, we must translate (or parse) this data into a format that Dart can comprehend in order to use it in our program.

- JSON Data Parsing: Now let's examine the JSON data that we obtained.

```
import 'dart:convert';

Future<Map<String, dynamic>> fetchData() async {
  final response = await http.get(Uri.parse('https://jsonplaceholder.typicode.com/todos/1'));

  if (response.statusCode == 200) {
    return json.decode(response.body);
  } else {
    throw Exception('Failed to load data');
```

}

}

In this example, the JSON string is transformed into a Dart map (a collection of key-value pairs) using the json.decode function.

### 6.3: Using Widgets to Show Fetched Data

After retrieving and analyzing the data, let's show it in our application. The UI can be updated with the retrieved data by using Stateful Widgets.

- **Data Display**: This is how the retrieved data might be shown in a widget.

```
class MyApp extends StatefulWidget {
  @override
  _MyAppState createState() => _MyAppState();
}


class _MyAppState extends State<MyApp> {
  Future<Map<String, dynamic>>? _futureData;
```

```
@override
void initState() {
  super.initState();
  _futureData = fetchData();
}


@override
Widget build(BuildContext context) {
  return MaterialApp(
    home: Scaffold(
      appBar: AppBar(title: Text('Fetch Data Example')),
      body: Center(
        child: FutureBuilder<Map<String, dynamic>>(
          future: _futureData,
          builder: (context, snapshot) {
            if (snapshot.connectionState == ConnectionState.waiting) {
              return CircularProgressIndicator();
            } else if (snapshot.hasError) {
              return Text('Error: ${snapshot.error}');
```

```
            } else {
                                    return Text('Title:
${snapshot.data?['title']}');
                }
            },
        ),
    ),
  ),
);
  }
}
```

In this example, the fetched data is handled using FutureBuilder. We display a loading spinner while the data is being fetched. We show the error if there is one. If not, the data is displayed.

## 6.4: Managing Errors and Loading States

Managing errors and loading states is crucial to creating a user-friendly application. You don't want users to become puzzled in the event that something goes wrong, or to be staring at a blank screen while waiting for data to load.

While the data is being fetched, display a loading indicator.

```
if (snapshot.connectionState == ConnectionState.waiting) {
  return CircularProgressIndicator();
}
```

To demonstrate that data is loading, this displays a spinning circle.

- Error State: When something goes wrong, display an error message.

```
else if (snapshot.hasError) {
  return Text('Error: ${snapshot.error}');
}
```

If a retrieval issue arises, this shows an error message.

- Success State: After the data has been successfully fetched, display it.

```
    else {
      return Text('Title: ${snapshot.data?['title']}');
    }
```

Once the data has been correctly loaded, this displays it.

This is the whole example, which handles the loading, error, and success states:

```
class MyApp extends StatefulWidget {
  @override
  _MyAppState createState() => _MyAppState();
}

class _MyAppState extends State<MyApp> {
  Future<Map<String, dynamic>>? _futureData;

  @override
  void initState() {
    super.initState();
    _futureData = fetchData();
  }
```

```dart
@override
Widget build(BuildContext context) {
  return MaterialApp(
    home: Scaffold(
      appBar: AppBar(title: Text('Fetch Data Example')),
      body: Center(
        child: FutureBuilder<Map<String, dynamic>>(
          future: _futureData,
          builder: (context, snapshot) {
            if (snapshot.connectionState == ConnectionState.waiting) {
              return CircularProgressIndicator();
            } else if (snapshot.hasError) {
              return Text('Error: ${snapshot.error}');
            } else {
              return Text('Title: ${snapshot.data?['title']}');
            }
          },
        ),
      ),
    ),
  );
}
```

}

These tools let you properly handle loading states and problems while retrieving, parsing, and displaying data from the internet within your application. Your app will become more dynamic and user-responsive as a result. With continued practice and experimentation, you'll become an expert in Flutter's asynchronous data handling!

# CHAPTER 7

# Navigation and Routing in Flutter

## 7.1: Using Navigator for Navigation

Consider yourself in a large amusement park, wanting to check out a variety of rides and attractions. Navigating through the many screens (or pages) in a Flutter application is similar to exploring an amusement park. Navigator is the tool we use to navigate between screens.

- Navigator: The Navigator facilitates screen switching, much like a map does when assisting with park navigation.

    Navigator.push(
      context,
        MaterialPageRoute(builder: (context) => SecondScreen()),
    );

Navigator.push in this case moves you from the screen you are currently on to the SecondScreen.

## 7.2: Using Push and Pop to Construct Navigation Stacks

Upon visiting several locations throughout the amusement park, you may find yourself wishing to return to your previous location. You can use push to navigate to a new screen in Flutter and pop to return to the previous screen.

- Push: This causes a new screen to be added to the top of the screen stack.

    Navigator.push(
      context,
        MaterialPageRoute(builder: (context) => SecondScreen()),
    );

The SecondScreen is added in this example on top of the active screen.

- Pop: This returns you to the previous screen by removing the top screen.

Navigator.pop(context);

In this example, you exit the current screen and return to the one before it.

## 7.3: Identified Paths and Navigational Debates

In certain cases, using names to navigate between screens is more convenient, particularly when your application has numerous displays. Named routes are in handy in this situation.

- Named Routes: Named routes function similarly to labels on various displays. These labels allow you to navigate.

    ```
    void main() {
      runApp(MaterialApp(
        initialRoute: '/',
    ```

```
  routes: {
    '/': (context) => HomeScreen(),
    '/second': (context) => SecondScreen(),
  },
));
}
```

The home screen (/) and the second screen (/second) are the two routes that are defined in this example.

- **Arguments for Navigation:** It's occasionally necessary to transfer data to a new screen. Arguments can be used for this purpose.

```
Navigator.pushNamed(
  context,
  '/second',
  arguments: 'Hello from the first screen!',
);

class SecondScreen extends StatelessWidget {
  @override
  Widget build(BuildContext context) {
```

```
    final    String    args    =
ModalRoute.of(context)?.settings.arguments    as
String;

    return Scaffold(
      appBar: AppBar(
        title: Text('Second Screen'),
      ),
      body: Center(
        child: Text(args),
      ),
    );
  }
}
```

In this instance, a message is sent to the SecondScreen and shown there.

## 7.4: Tabs and Bottom Navigation Bars

Let's say you wish to have easy access to the rides, food vendors, and activities in the amusement park. To generate a comparable user experience in your app, you may use tabs and bottom navigation bars in Flutter.

- Bottom Navigation Bar: This useful tool makes it simple to navigate between sections.

```
class MyApp extends StatefulWidget {
  @override
  _MyAppState createState() => _MyAppState();
}

class _MyAppState extends State<MyApp> {
  int _selectedIndex = 0;

  static const List<Widget> _widgetOptions = <Widget>[
    Text('Home'),
    Text('Search'),
    Text('Profile'),
  ];

  void _onItemTapped(int index) {
    setState(() {
      _selectedIndex = index;
```

```
    });
}


@override
Widget build(BuildContext context) {
  return MaterialApp(
    home: Scaffold(
      appBar: AppBar(
        title: Text('Bottom Navigation Bar Example'),
      ),
      body: Center(
        child: _widgetOptions.elementAt(_selectedIndex),
      ),
      bottomNavigationBar: BottomNavigationBar(
        items: const <BottomNavigationBarItem>[
          BottomNavigationBarItem(
            icon: Icon(Icons.home),
            label: 'Home',
          ),
          BottomNavigationBarItem(
            icon: Icon(Icons.search),
            label: 'Search',
```

```
      ),
      BottomNavigationBarItem(
        icon: Icon(Icons.person),
        label: 'Profile',
      ),
    ],
    currentIndex: _selectedIndex,
    onTap: _onItemTapped,
      ),
    ),
  );
  }
}
```

Here, the Home, Search, and Profile areas can be navigated between using the bottom navigation bar.

- Another tool for grouping distinct portions of your software is tabs.

```
class MyTabbedApp extends StatelessWidget {
  @override
```

```
Widget build(BuildContext context) {
  return MaterialApp(
    home: DefaultTabController(
      length: 3,
      child: Scaffold(
        appBar: AppBar(
          title: Text('Tabs Example'),
          bottom: TabBar(
            tabs: [
              Tab(icon: Icon(Icons.directions_car)),
              Tab(icon: Icon(Icons.directions_transit)),
              Tab(icon: Icon(Icons.directions_bike)),
            ],
          ),
        ),
        body: TabBarView(
          children: [
            Icon(Icons.directions_car),
            Icon(Icons.directions_transit),
            Icon(Icons.directions_bike),
          ],
        ),
      ),
```

```
        ),
      );
    }
}
```

In this example, you can alternate between three icons: a bike, a bus, and an automobile using the tabs.

If you know how to use routing and navigation, you can make a Flutter application that has the vibe of a well-run theme park. Users may navigate and explore the app's various areas with ease. If you practice a lot, you'll become an expert navigator in Flutter very soon!

# CHAPTER 8

# Animations and Transitions

## 8.1: Comprehending Flutter's Animation

Assume you're present at a magic show. A hat that grows larger or a ball that changes color are just two examples of the astounding ways the magician can make objects move and alter. Animations in Flutter are similar to that magic. They easily alter the elements on the screen to give your software a lively, entertaining appearance.

- Fundamentals of Animation: Animations cause changes to occur gradually over time. Rather than emerging abruptly, something may gradually become visible or flow gently from one area to another.

```
// Example of a simple animation that changes color over time
class ColorChangeAnimation extends StatefulWidget {
```

```dart
  @override
  _ColorChangeAnimationState createState() =>
_ColorChangeAnimationState();
}


class _ColorChangeAnimationState extends
State<ColorChangeAnimation>
    with SingleTickerProviderStateMixin {
  late AnimationController _controller;
  late Animation<Color?> _animation;

  @override
  void initState() {
    super.initState();
    _controller = AnimationController(
      duration: const Duration(seconds: 2),
      vsync: this,
    );

    _animation = ColorTween(begin: Colors.blue,
end: Colors.red)
        .animate(_controller);
```

```dart
    _controller.repeat(reverse: true);
  }

  @override
  Widget build(BuildContext context) {
    return AnimatedBuilder(
      animation: _animation,
      builder: (context, child) {
        return Container(
          width: 100,
          height: 100,
          color: _animation.value,
        );
      },
    );
  }

  @override
  void dispose() {
    _controller.dispose();
    super.dispose();
  }
}
```

This example shows how to easily alter a box's color from blue to red and back again.

## 8.2: Making Simple Animations using AnimatedContainer

Let's begin by utilizing AnimatedContainer to create a basic animation. This is comparable to when a magician subtly alters an object, such as by changing the color or size of a box.

- AnimatedContainer: This type of container animates changes to its width, height, color, and other parameters automatically.

```
class SimpleAnimation extends StatefulWidget {
  @override
  _SimpleAnimationState createState() =>
      _SimpleAnimationState();
}
```

```dart
class _SimpleAnimationState extends State<SimpleAnimation> {
  bool _isBig = false;

  @override
  Widget build(BuildContext context) {
    return Scaffold(
      appBar: AppBar(
        title: Text('Simple Animation'),
      ),
      body: Center(
        child: AnimatedContainer(
          width: _isBig ? 200 : 100,
          height: _isBig ? 200 : 100,
          color: _isBig ? Colors.blue : Colors.red,
          duration: Duration(seconds: 1),
          curve: Curves.easeInOut,
          child: GestureDetector(
            onTap: () {
              setState(() {
                _isBig = !_isBig;
              });
            },
```

```
            child: Center(
              child: Text(
                'Tap me!',
                style: TextStyle(color: Colors.white),
              ),
            ),
          ),
        ),
      ),
    );
  }
}
```

In this example, we make a box that responds to touch by changing both its size and color. When you tap it again, it shrinks and turns red again, then gets bigger and bluer.

## 8.3: Using Animations and AnimatedBuilder

You can use AnimatedBuilder to build more intricate animations. This is comparable to seeing a magician execute a complex trick that takes several steps.

- **AnimatedBuilder:** By joining several animations together, AnimatedBuilder enables you to create more intricate animations.

```dart
class ComplexAnimation extends StatefulWidget {
  @override
    _ComplexAnimationState createState() => _ComplexAnimationState();
}

class _ComplexAnimationState extends State<ComplexAnimation>
    with SingleTickerProviderStateMixin {
  late AnimationController _controller;
  late Animation<double> _animation;

  @override
  void initState() {
    super.initState();
    _controller = AnimationController(
      duration: const Duration(seconds: 2),
      vsync: this,
    );
```

```
    _animation = Tween<double>(begin: 0, end: 300).animate(_controller);

    _controller.repeat(reverse: true);
}

@override
Widget build(BuildContext context) {
  return Scaffold(
    appBar: AppBar(
      title: Text('Complex Animation'),
    ),
    body: Center(
      child: AnimatedBuilder(
        animation: _animation,
        builder: (context, child) {
          return Container(
            width: _animation.value,
            height: _animation.value,
            color: Colors.green,
          );
        },
```

```
      ),
    ),
  );
}


@override
void dispose() {
  _controller.dispose();
  super.dispose();
  }
}
```

We make a green box in this example that expands and shrinks gradually.

## 8.4: Producing Personalized Animations

You may occasionally desire to make original animations of your own. It's similar to when a magician creates a whole new act.

- Custom Animations: By combining various

animation techniques, you may produce unique animations.

```dart
class CustomAnimation extends StatefulWidget {
  @override
    _CustomAnimationState createState() => _CustomAnimationState();
}

class _CustomAnimationState extends State<CustomAnimation>
    with SingleTickerProviderStateMixin {
  late AnimationController _controller;
  late Animation<double> _sizeAnimation;
  late Animation<Color?> _colorAnimation;

  @override
  void initState() {
    super.initState();
    _controller = AnimationController(
      duration: const Duration(seconds: 3),
      vsync: this,
    );
```

```
  _sizeAnimation = Tween<double>(begin: 50, end:
200).animate(
    CurvedAnimation(
      parent: _controller,
      curve: Curves.bounceInOut,
    ),
  );

  _colorAnimation = ColorTween(begin:
Colors.purple, end: Colors.orange)
      .animate(_controller);

  _controller.repeat(reverse: true);
}

@override
Widget build(BuildContext context) {
  return Scaffold(
    appBar: AppBar(
      title: Text('Custom Animation'),
    ),
    body: Center(
```

```
      child: AnimatedBuilder(
        animation: _controller,
        builder: (context, child) {
          return Container(
            width: _sizeAnimation.value,
            height: _sizeAnimation.value,
            color: _colorAnimation.value,
          );
        },
      ),
    ),
  );
}

@override
void dispose() {
  _controller.dispose();
  super.dispose();
}
}
```

In this example, we make a box that bounces and changes color and size.

You may increase the enjoyment and engagement of your Flutter app by mastering these animation techniques. Your software can come to life with animations, giving it a mystical appearance akin to a magician's illusions. To make incredible animations, never stop learning and trying new things!

# CHAPTER 9

# Writing Unit Tests for Flutter Apps

**9.1: Testing Is Essential to Flutter Development**

Consider yourself constructing a LEGO palace. To prevent your fortress from collapsing, you want to ensure that every component is sturdy and solid. In Flutter development, testing is akin to inspecting every LEGO piece and connection to ensure your program functions flawlessly.

Why Test? Testing enables us to identify and address errors in our code before users do. It makes sure our program operates as intended and guards against glitches or failures.

1. Identify bugs early: Problems are easier to solve when discovered early on.
2. Tests ensure that your software continues to function properly even after you make changes.

## 9.2: Using a test package to set up a testing environment

Setting up a testing environment is necessary before we begin testing. This is similar to organizing all of your LEGO parts and building instructions before you begin construction.

Installing the test package: Initially, make sure your project has the test package. Test-writing and execution tools are included in this package.

```
dev_dependencies:
  test: ^1.16.0
```

Run flutter pub to install the package after adding this.

Making a Test File: The next step is to make a test file in which your tests will be written.

```
test/my_test.dart
```

## 9.3: Formulating Unit Tests for Logic and Widgets

Writing unit tests is similar to double-checking that every LEGO piece and connector fit together precisely. You can ensure that every component of your program functions properly by using unit tests.

- **Function Testing:** Let's begin with a basic illustration of a function test.

  ```
  // lib/calculate.dart
  int add(int a, int b) {
    return a + b;
  }
  ```

  ```
  // test/calculate_test.dart
  import 'package:flutter_test/flutter_test.dart';
  import '../lib/calculate.dart';
  ```

```dart
void main() {
  test('adds two numbers', () {
    expect(add(2, 3), 5);
  });
}
```

We are evaluating a function that adds two numbers in this example. We verify that add(2, 3) yields a value of 5.

- **Examining a Widget**: Let's test a basic widget now.

```dart
// lib/my_widget.dart
import 'package:flutter/material.dart';

class MyWidget extends StatelessWidget {
  final String title;

  MyWidget({required this.title});

  @override
  Widget build(BuildContext context) {
    return MaterialApp(
      home: Scaffold(
```

```
      appBar: AppBar(
        title: Text(title),
      ),
    ),
  );
 }
}
```

```
// test/my_widget_test.dart
import 'package:flutter/material.dart';
import 'package:flutter_test/flutter_test.dart';
import '../lib/my_widget.dart';

void main() {
  testWidgets('MyWidget has a title', (WidgetTester tester) async {
     await tester.pumpWidget(MyWidget(title: 'Test Title'));

    final titleFinder = find.text('Test Title');
    expect(titleFinder, findsOneWidget);
  });
```

We are trying a title-displayed widget in this example. We verify that the title appears on the screen accurately.

## 9.4: Using and Troubleshooting Tests

Testing is similar to going over each LEGO piece to make sure it fits and functions as it should. You are able to debug and correct any issues that may arise.

- Executing Tests: Type the following command into your terminal to begin running your tests:

    flutter test

- Debugging Tests: Flutter will display an error message explaining the reason for the failure of a test. After that, you can return to your code, address the problem, and rerun the tests.

    An Example of an Error Message

Expected: <5>

Actual: <4>

This notice means that, although the test was expecting a score of 5, the outcome was only 4. With this knowledge, you can identify and address the issue in your code.

A failed test example would be:

```
test('subtracts two numbers', () {
    expect(subtract(5, 3), 3); // This will fail because 5 - 3 is not 3
});
```

Adjust the anticipated outcome to remedy the error:

```
test('subtracts two numbers', () {
    expect(subtract(5, 3), 2); // Corrected the expected result to 2
});
```

You can make sure your Flutter app is robust and stable, much like a well-built LEGO castle, by learning the value of testing and how to set up, develop, and run tests. Cheers to your testing!

# CHAPTER 10

## Deploying Your Flutter App

**10.1: Preparing Your App for Distribution**

Let's say you have constructed the most amazing LEGO castle ever and you are eager to show your friends. In Flutter, you have to get your app ready for release before you can publish it to the public. This entails preparing it for universal use.

- Build for Release: This stage is similar to finishing the LEGO castle by making sure everything is flawless.

- Flutter Command: You use certain commands to build your app for release.

Regarding Android

flutter build apk --release

Regarding iOS:

flutter build ios --release

Optimizations: Flutter guarantees fast and seamless operation of your application. It makes your app faster and smaller by removing unnecessary extras.

## 10.2: Uploading to the iOS App Store

Let's now imagine that you wish to exhibit your iPhone-using buddies at your LEGO fortress. You must submit your program to the program Store, which functions as a sizable app store, in order to accomplish this.

Apple Developer Account: To begin with, you must have one. This is analogous to entering the toy store with a membership card.

1. Register: Apple Developer is the place to register.

2. Cost: Like a membership fee, there is an annual charge.
3. Getting Your App Ready: Make sure your software satisfies all standards before submitting it to the store.
4. Xcode: To prepare your app, use Xcode on a Mac. Comparable to the unique box required to package your LEGO fortress is Xcode.

Launch Xcode and open your project by typing

open ios/Runner.xcworkspace

5. Configure all the required parameters, such as the name and icon for your app.
6. Getting Your App Submitted: You submit your app to the App Store once it's all set.
7. App Store Connect: This is where you can administer your application.
8. Visit the App Store Connect page.
9. Complete all of the app's information fields.

10. Apps can be uploaded via Xcode.

## 10.3: Introducing Android to the Google Play Store

Now let's show off your LEGO fortress to your Android-using friends. You place your program in the Google Play shop, another sizable app shop, to do this.

Google Play Developer Account: Prior to anything else, you must have one.

1. Sign Up: The Google Play Console is where you may register.
2. Cost: There is a one-time enrollment charge.
3. Getting Your App Ready: Make sure your app is ready before submitting it to the store.

Keystore: This is akin to a unique key that locks the LEGO castle box, allowing you to be the only one with access.

Establish a keystore with

keytool -genkey -v -keystore my-release-key.jks -keyalg

RSA -keysize 2048 -validity 10000 -alias my-key-alias

Safely store this keystore file.

- Construct the APK: To create the APK (Android Package) file, use Flutter.

flutter build apk --release

1. Uploading Your App: At this point, you are able to submit your app to the Google Play Store.
2. Use the Google Play Console to manage your app.
3. Visit the Play Console on Google.
4. Enter all the details about your app, including screenshots and a description.
5. Put the APK file you created online.

## 10.4: Comprehending App Store Policies

Similar to how regulations exist in toy stores to ensure safety and equity, app stores similarly have policies that you must abide with.

iOS App Store Guidelines:

1. Content: Verify that your software is suitable for users of all ages.
2. Functionality: There should be no issues and your program should function as intended.
3. Privacy: Honor the data and privacy of users.
4. All of the rules are available to read here: The App Store Rules from Apple.

Android Google Play Guidelines:

1. Content: Steer clear of offensive material.
2. Functionality: Your application must be reliable and error-free.
3. Privacy: Preserve users' personal information.
4. All of the rules are available to read here: Developer Policy for Google Play.

Understanding and adhering to these rules can help you ensure that your software is dependable, secure, and entertaining for users of all skill levels.

# ABOUT THE AUTHOR

One well-known author and thought leader in the IT space is Taylor Royce. Over the course of a two-decade career, Royce has established himself as a reliable source for tech trend analysis and forecasting, bringing complicated technological ideas within reach of a wide audience. Royce is well-known for his perceptive and innovative work, which spans a broad range of subjects such as blockchain, artificial intelligence, cybersecurity, and the Internet of Things (IoT).

Royce's interest in technology started while he studied computer science, where his early curiosity with the possibilities of computing systems established the groundwork for a long-lasting and intense involvement with the tech industry. Royce's practical expertise in a range of tech professions, from software development to strategic consulting, combined with his academic background to provide him a thorough understanding of the inner workings of the sector.

Taylor Royce has penned multiple best-selling books and contributed to many esteemed tech journals throughout the course of a busy writing career. These pieces are distinguished by their precision, extensive investigation, and capacity to reduce complicated concepts into understandable insights for both IT fans and corporations. Royce's writings have been translated into other languages, demonstrating their popularity and influence around the world.

Aside from writing, Royce frequently appears as a guest on tech-related podcasts and webinars and is in high demand as a speaker at international tech conferences. Because of his increased visibility, Royce has solidified his reputation as a leading expert in the IT sector, frequently consulted for his knowledgeable opinions on cutting-edge technology and their social ramifications.

Royce's work largely addresses the moral and societal ramifications of technological progress. Royce, who promotes ethical tech creation and use, stresses the significance of tackling problems like data privacy, the digital gap, and the moral application of artificial intelligence. Royce's contributions are certain to be both educational and in line with the larger objective of using technology for the greater benefit because of this balanced viewpoint.

Beyond just writing and speaking, Taylor Royce has a significant impact on a number of IT education initiatives and actively mentors upcoming tech workers. This emphasis on developing the next wave of tech innovators demonstrates a commitment to the equitable and sustainable development of the tech sector.

All things considered, Taylor Royce is a well-known personality in the field of technology writing, renowned for his ability to combine technical know-how with careful analysis and a vision of a time when technology will meaningfully and morally serve humankind.

www.ingramcontent.com/pod-product-compliance
Lightning Source LLC
Chambersburg PA
CBHW070112230526
45472CB00004B/1226